I0021476

HOW THE INTERNET WORKS & THE WEB DEVELOPMENT PROCESS

Section 1:

How the

Internet Works

The Internet Overview

Before we can venture into the world of web development it's important to have a fundamental understanding of how the internet works. Meaning what's happening behind the scenes. When we type a web address into our web browser or send a file or email to a recipient this information will be very useful as we explore the concepts covered in this book to think of it in its simplest terms. The Internet is a network of cables that facilitates the transmission of data packets the network is extremely vast and spreads globally across five hundred and fifty thousand miles of hidden cables under the ocean. To keep the world connected this page provides a graphical illustration of how complex the network of cables that power the internet really is a data packet contains the information being transmitted such as an email file or web page in raw text format and also the location of the sender and the recipient of the data packet. You can think of the location of a recipient or sender is the physical address of your residence or a phone number. No two residences have the same address and no two people have the same phone number. The same is true for internet addresses also known as an IP address an IP is a string of numbers separated by periods that identifies each computer that is connected to a network or the Internet. For example the IP address for Google dot coms web server is 7 for dot 1 2 5 2 2 4 dot 7 2 each Web site has its own unique IP address we'll discuss how this IP translates into Google dot com later in this book. Let's take a look at an example of an email data packet as we can see the data packet consists of three parts the header the header identifies the sender and the receivers IP address. It also specifies the protocol which we will explore later on it indicates the payload which in this case includes the actual email that is being transmitted. Lastly it includes a trailer which indicates that the package is complete and there is no further data for transmission. The speed at which data packets can be transmitted over a network is determined by bandwidth band width transmission capacity is measured by rate the bit rate is the number of bits per second that a digital network can transmit another measure of data transmission speed is latencyr. Let's talk about an example if you want to send a four megabyte MP three file to a friend through an email attachment in four seconds you would require a bit rate of eight megabytes per second. This is because 8 million bits equals one megabyte now with billions of people connected to the internet at any given moment. It goes without saying that the Internet is comprised of hundreds of thousands of networks and links billions of devices together globally with this level of connectivity. You might be wondering how each individual network device can efficiently and accurately interpret and read data packets from various unique senders. Well you can think of the Internet is an architecture expressed in a set of protocols a protocol is a well-established set of rules and standards used to communicate between machines. We've already touched on one protocol the IP the IP is used to route information to the proper address and make sure that the data packets are sent to the intended recipient. Note that the IP protocol does not facilitate physical connections between computers to transmit data packets the TTP protocol is intended for that purpose the TTP protocol make sure that transmitted data packets are received without any missing information if it's determined that the data packet is missing data DCP will request that the sender sends them some other protocols that will explore in this book include HDP HDD P S S M P and FCP.

The HTTP Protocol

The GDP and GDP as protocols are very relevant to this book. These protocols define how your Internet browser communicates with the web server to display your website. Keep in mind that a web page and its contents are transmitted in the form of data packets just like any other type of file. You can think of a web server as a computer that hosts a Web site or web application and is configured to accept remote connections with Internet users and relay data through the HDP or HDP as protocol. Note that HDP stands for Hypertext Transfer Protocol while HDTV S stands for Hypertext Transfer Protocol Secure let's start with taking a closer look at the HDP protocol when we type a web address into web browser. So for example www dot Google dot com our modem will communicates with Internet service provider to translate Web address into a numerical IP address. This is done through DNS domain name servers. These are administered by ISP or Internet service provider the domain name server is a list of domain names and their corresponding IP address.

Sometimes your ISP may not be able to locate the IP in their DNS records. your ISP would take it a step further and query other authoritative DNS servers for the IP once the IP is found. It sends data back to your web browser. Your web browser then sends a GET request to the IP address and if the request is successful the contents of the Web page are delivered through data packets and displayed in your web browser a GET request for www dot Google dot com would look something like this get and then the HDTV protocol and the name of the host. This is the IP address for the Google dot com Web page. If the GET request is successful Google dot com will send back packets with the HDMI code for the home page HD CML is the programming language that instructs your web browser on how to present the page it tells the browser where each object text images videos should be displayed and where they're located.

The HTTPS Protocol

The HDP has protocol is a more secure method of data transmission than the HDP protocol the data packets that transfer back and forth between your browser and the Web site's server are not encrypted with the standard HDP protocol. This means they are in plain text and if they were intercepted by an intruder all the information would be readily visible with HDTV s all the data packets are encrypted using SSL or secure socket layer or less transport layer security. This means that the information contained within the data packets are coded and can only be interpreted if certain conditions are met. The actual encryption and decryption process is quite technical and beyond the scope of this book an SSL layer can be created by installing a security certificate on the web server that hosts the website a security certificate can be purchased from a reputable vendor that will verify information about the domain and registrant if the registrant of the domain name is a business. Then additional validation documents may also be required. The verification process differs from each vendor and more reputable vendors will likely require more information. There are also different types of certificates a high level security certificate it is known is the Extended Validation certificate or evey it generally takes the most time to acquire and requires very detailed validation. Prior to issuance diagram offers an illustration of how the encryption process works when a website visitor visits an SSL protected Web site. The SSL certificate installed on the web server automatically creates an encrypted connection with the visitors web browser. This is called the SSL handshake. Once the connection is established a padlock icon and HDP has prefix appear in the visitors web browser this generally means the site is safe to share personal details. It's important to make sure the SSL certificate is issued by a well recognized authority before sharing sensitive information the SSL encryption is a 2048 bit encryption which is virtually unbreakable.

The SMTP Protocol and Local Mail

The S.M. teepee or simple mail transfer protocol is another protocol that you will almost certainly encounter as a web developer after your web application has been developed you will need to communicate with your customers through email management and setup can be quite complex especially when your email list exceeds thousands of subscribers. There are many options available when configuring email clients in servers it's important to thoroughly understand the email exchange process before diving into complex and intricate area of development SMP is the standard protocol for electronic mail or email transmission. It's important to note that there are two types of email exchange scenarios. First the sender and receiver are exchanging emails or originating from the same domain. So for example Jane Gmail dot com is sending an email to Joe at Gmail dot com. This is known as local mail delivery in the second scenario the center's domain is different than the recipient. For example Jane at G.M. dot com is sending an email to Bob at yahoo dot com in this case. The email is transmitted externally or outside of the local network. Depending on the type of email exchange the path to delivery will be quite different. We'll start with local mail delivery in this case the sender sends the email from his or her workstation either through a Web based mail service or from a locally installed email client such as Microsoft Outlook either way. The email is sent to the outgoing SMP server that resides on the email provider's server. In this case Gmail the SMP server has a variety of tasks it checks the data packets for header information as you might recall the header information in a packet contains the sender and recipient of the packet the SMP server would determine this email is intended for local mail delivery because the originating email domain Jane a G.M. dot com is the same as the recipient Joe at G.M. dot com. This is done by separating the first part of the email from the email extension and comparing the results the SMP server would easily determine that they are both Gmail accounts in this case Gmail is outgoing SMP server would hold the emails internally in the email storage.

This is until Joe connects to the server and downloads the mail waiting for him. The emails are downloaded using the pop 3 protocol this protocol is responsible for transmitting stored email messages to the designated recipient the pop 3 server typically requires authentication such as a username and password to connect and download the email messages in storage if Joe is using an email client and downloads the messages from the pop 3 server. The messages are transferred to Joe's computer and deleted from the server the pop 3 server is not ideal for recipients who may use multiple computers to download their email messages some businesses opt to use an eye map server to handle email storage instead of pop 3 with a map email messages stay on the server even after they are downloaded by the recipient's email client.

Outbound Mail Delivery

Now let's talk about the second scenario a more complex situation arises when the recipient's e-mail server is located outside the local network so the sender. In example is Jane a G.M. dot com and the recipient is Bob at yahoo dot com. In this case the SMP server needs to locate the recipient's e-mail server you might recall that when we discussed the HDP protocol your web browser communicated with the DNS server of your ISP to locate the IP address of the web server hosting the website you wanted to view when sending an external email message. Something very similar happens your SMP server will look at the extension of the recipient's address in this case yahoo dot com. It will then communicate with the ISP DNS server to locate the IP address of yahoo dot coms mail server remember the IP address identifies the location of the destination server which in this case is yahoo dot com once we have the destination ip address the SMP server will connect with the destination email server at this point the destination server will run a variety of spam filters to ensure the message is not junk mail once it's determined that the message is safe for delivery the destination server will keep the message in Joe's email store until Joe connects to his email provider's email server and downloads the message using either pop 3 or Ima.

Network Basics - LAN and WAN

Now we can take a look at the mechanisms that allow or restrict the movement of these packets using network routers firewalls import configurations we'll start with local area networks a local area network is best described as a group of computers that share a common communications line within a relatively small area a LAN is typically confined to a single room building or group of buildings let's explore how the land is formed in some important considerations to illustrate the structure of a local area network. We'll start with the most basic network configuration when we first sign up for Internet access with our local ISP the ISP issues us a modem this modem is connected to our ISP using a coaxial cable or DSL phone line this cable connection allows us to transmit data packets over the Internet as we learned earlier technically we can now take a computer and connect it directly to the modem using an ether net cable in this case the IP address assigned to the modem by our ISP would resolve directly to our computer we're now connected and can send emails browse the internet and transfer files. This is a great start but there are some important issues we have neglected in this type of setup. The first major issue is security and the second is network expand ability. First our computers operating system whether Windows Mac OS or Linux is a very complex software with many applications it's open to security vulnerabilities that can be exploited over an internet connection hackers commonly look for security issues in software and exploit these vulnerabilities when found by connecting directly to your modem. Hackers can transmit data requests much more easily to your computer and determine if any vulnerabilities do exist secondly say we wanted to split our internet connection so that two or three computers and other devices such as printers and mobile phones can simultaneously be connected a modem only allows a single Ethernet cable or DSL line connection in order to split the connection we would need a router by connecting the modem to a router. All devices connected to the rotor can access the modem and therefore the Internet the router provides a local unique IP address to each connected device though they would still have the same external or public IP the rotor would then analyze all data packets traveling through the network and direct them to the appropriate locations whether within the LAN or destined for the Internet. The router directs the email to the Web to the wide area network for outbound delivery John has also sent a print job to a printer attached to the network through the router the router knows to keep the data packets associated with the print job within the local network it sends the packets to the printer for Bob receives an incoming MP three file transfer and the router directs the file to Bob's computer using his locally assigned IP address Kim is browsing the internet and the router is directing incoming and outgoing each TTP requests to Kim's web browser Su's tablet is connected to the router through Wi-Fi the router has assigned Su's tablet a local IP address just like any other device since Sue is on the Internet using Facebook the router is relaying HDP packets from Soo's web browser to Facebook Web server when or wide area network is simply a more complex network that spans across much larger geographic areas such as cities states and nations we've already discussed how vast the Internet network is and its global reach wide area networks are typically built by Internet service providers to provide connections for local area networks of their customers to the Internet since the Internet is a worldwide network of interconnected computer networks it's the largest when in existence.

Network Ports and Firewalls

Now that we have a better understanding of local area networks and wide area networks and the role of a network rotor let's explore basic security configurations in the previous lecture. We introduced the role of a roader in setting up a network. We also suggested that connecting your modem directly to your computer was not a good practice. Well not only does a router help you connect multiple devices to your network it also significantly enhances your network security. If configured correctly even if you only have one computer hooked up hooked up to the router routers allow you to control the data packets that are allowed to enter your local network from the Internet. The reason is because all incoming and outgoing data packets must travel through designated ports on your router a network port within the context of the Internet can be thought of as a data pipeline that is configured on your networks rotor ports can be open or closed to allow or restrict the movement of data packets associated with various protocols that we discussed such as HDTV s MTV POP 3 And FTB port numbers are assigned a numerical value when created. For example port 80 generally handles incoming and outgoing data requests transmitted through HDP viewing and hosting Web pages. Another example is port 25 which handles data transmitted through SMP for sending emails port 21 is used for exchanging files over the file transfer protocol or FTB rotors also have built in firewalls. These are known as hardware firewalls and are very effective in protecting your network security a firewall is a system designed to prevent unauthorized access to or from a network. They can be customized to meet your networks needs. In addition to a hardware firewall a software firewall can also be added for an additional layer of security most operating systems come with built. Come with a built in software firewall such as Windows firewall a software firewall prevents data packets containing malicious content from entering your network. This type of firewall can be installed on your computer if there isn't one present already firewall configurations can block certain ports from transmitting data or block specified applications from transmitting data packets. We can say that the firewall on computer does not allow the application Skype icy hue or vibrate to communicate with the Internet if the user attempts to transmit data packets through applications. They will be blocked by the systems software firewall . The computer has no firewall the user is attempting to send an email to Bob using SMP port 25 the email data packet successfully travels past the router and through the modem to the sender's ISP the ISP successfully delivers the message to Bob's email server Bob is at work in attempting to connect it to his email provider server to check his email he doesn't realize that his employer has blocked Pt. 1 1 0 the default port for incoming mail over pop 3 as a result he is unable to receive his email messages. Note that software firewalls are not as effective as hardware firewalls. Much of the effectiveness of a software firewall depends on the overall configuration of your operating system and all the applications that are installed. Sometimes downloading a Trojan or a virus by mistake can open a backdoor into a network leaving a software firewall meaningless in the line of defense. A hardware firewall on the other hand is not as vulnerable because it is not affected by security threats installed on a computer within the local area network.

Section 2:

The Web Development Process - An Overview

Web Development Process Overview

we'll be conducting an overview of the entire web development process. Once the overview is complete we'll take an in-depth look at each step. We'll be following this process during the book and also in the development of the Web sites we create as part of the tutorials. It's very important to have a thorough understanding of each part of this process so you know exactly what we're doing each step of the way. Also making mistakes in the early stages can sometimes lead to significant issues later on. So keep that in mind and let's get started. Step one is to plan and create a flow diagram of your Web site. Step two is to determine your system requirements and preferred hosting solution Step three is to choose a domain name and register it the domain name is what people will use to access your Web site. It's your web address step for is to configure a local testing server Step five is to configure a production environment a live web server Step six is to install and set up an FTE service Step seven is to develop the front end of your web application using HMO CSX bootstrap java script and Jake Query Step eight is to set up a database using my sequel and P HP my admin my sequel in P HP my admin are database management tools they enable us to add access and manage database content step 9 is to interact with your database using P HP for dynamic functionality and user interactivity Step ten is to upload your website using an FTE P service Step Eleven is to configure DNS records so your domain name translates into your web pages IP address and finally step 12 is to configure a custom email address on your domain.

Section 3: Planning a Website

Web Application Planning Overview

Step one in the development process is to plan the flow of your Web site or application. It's very important to create a clear and concise plan of your Web site prior to development. The first step to planning is establishing the purpose of your Web site. For example is the site meant more for informational purposes such as showcasing a product or service. Or is it meant to interact with your users and dynamically adapt to their preferences and browsing habits. This is an important consideration because it will ultimately determine the infrastructure your site needs in order to accomplish your goals. If you're still unclear on the difference between a static informational site and a dynamic interactive site let's talk about an example of each one the site flex Zilla dot com sells a specialty garden hose product. This site is fairly simple. It showcases the product and provide some information to potential buyers the site does not interact or require any information from us besides a basic contact form nor does it customize its interface. Based on our browsing behaviors it's a static site with a few pages intended to inform customers on its product and this is the contact form fairly basic interaction. Now let's talk about a much more complex dynamic web site such as Amazon.com this Web site sells over 200 million products in thousands of different product categories we can see on the home page a variety of different types of products the site has a customer portal that allows us to sign in and configure settings that will custom tailor the shopping experience based on our interests Amazon also likely has a variety of other seamless tracking mechanisms to monitor our browsing behavior and display products that we would most likely purchase. This is a truly dynamic web site that interacts with its users to customize the browsing experience as you probably guessed. If your intention was to create a dynamic user interactive web application your system configuration and resource requirements would be entirely different than a static Web site we'll discuss the differences and in requirements. As we progressed through the book once you've established a purpose and goals of your site you can begin mapping out a flowchart of the site's navigation   flow chart is simply a hierarchical structure of each page and its interactions with other pages on your Web site. Let's talk about a very basic site structure for a sample real estate brokerages Web site. we have a home page. it is the first page that loads when a visitor access is the domain an about us page which will display information about the brokerage listings page which will showcase property listings organized by state on for sub pages. So for states and property listings pertaining to each state a sub page is lower on the Web site hierarchy than top level pages. And lastly a blog in contact page as you can see this is a very simple structure for demonstration purposes.

www.ingramcontent.com/pod-product-compliance
Lightning Source LLC
Chambersburg PA
CBHW061059050326
40690CB00012B/2669